THE
1992 ELECTION

Gene Brown

THE MILLBROOK PRESS

Brookfield, Connecticut

Published by The Millbrook Press
2 Old New Milford Road
Brookfield, CT 06804
© 1992 Blackbirch Graphics, Inc.
First Edition
5 4 3 2 1

Created and produced in association with Blackbirch Graphics.
Series Editor: Bruce S. Glassman

Library of Congress Cataloging-in-Publication Data
Brown, Gene.
   The 1992 Election/Gene Brown.
      p.   cm. — (Headliners)
   Includes bibliographical references and index.
   Summary: Discusses the issues, primaries, candidates, personalities, and
outcome of the 1992 presidential election, in a format that explains the
process and the problems of presidential campaigns.
      1. Presidents—United States—Election—1992—Juvenile literature.
2. Presidents—United States—Election—Juvenile literature. [1. Presi-
dents—Election. 2. Politics, Practical.] I. Title. II. Series.
   ISBN 1-56294-080-5   (lib. bdg.)
   JK526 1992c
   324.973'0928—dc20   92-19963
                                                                 CIP
                                                                  AC

Contents

Bill Clinton and Al Gore celebrate their victory on Election Day.

The Winners!

Some called it a "landslide." Others called it a "strong mandate." Whatever it was, on November 3, 1992, American voters sent a clear message to their leaders that they wanted change in Washington.

Bill Clinton had promised that change. He had also made the economy the major campaign issue, which proved to be the winning strategy. As a moderate southerner, Clinton recaptured the southern vote for the Democrats and successfully convinced the rest of the country that he was a "new kind of leader" at the head of a new kind of Democratic party. He thus managed to defeat incumbent Republican president George Bush, who had seemed invincible only a year before.

But 1992 was an extraordinary election year. It saw the second largest vote in history for a third-party candidate. And voter turnout was exceptionally high. All across the country, Americans who had not voted in years came out to have their voices heard. Millions of new voters were registered, and America's youth seemed energized to once again participate in the election process.

The "new Democratic party" had finally won favor with Americans. When it was all over, Clinton had a hundred more electoral votes than he needed to win, and he had received 43 percent of the popular vote. As rigorous as his campaign was, however, it would seem easy compared with what he needed to accomplish in the next four years.

Chapter 1

Shaping the '92 Campaign

Alittle over a year before the 1992 presidential election, things could not have looked better for George Bush. On March 6, 1991, he stood in total triumph before a joint session of Congress. Senators and members of the House of Representatives proudly waved American flags and yelled his name over and over.

The president was reporting to Congress on the victory over Iraq in Operation Desert Storm. Americans had watched on television as American "smart" bombs and Patriot missiles destroyed the enemy. The war over Kuwait had been short, and allied casualties few.

Unlike the war in Vietnam twenty-five years before, the country was almost fully behind the president once the fighting started. In fact, some polls showed that 90 percent of the American people approved of the way Bush was doing his job. Even the popular Ronald Reagan had never scored that high.

In the summer of 1991, with the glow of Desert Storm still radiating, President Bush claimed yet another foreign-policy victory. This one, emanating from Eastern Europe, ended a threat that went back more than a generation.

For forty years, Americans had seen communism as the most serious danger facing the United States. The Cold

George Bush
went from
unprecedented
popularity to
great disfavor
in a matter
of months.

Opposite:
In June 1991, a gigantic ticker-tape parade in New York City honored American troops who served in the Persian Gulf War.

War often threatened to turn hot. With each side pointing nuclear missiles at the other, such a war had the potential to destroy the human race.

As vice president, Bush had spoken out for President Reagan's tough stand on the Soviet Union. As president, he continued Reagan's approach of "standing up" to communism. Like Reagan, he also supported efforts by Soviet leader Mikhail Gorbachev to increase freedom behind the Iron Curtain.

By the summer of 1991, with the beginning of the presidential election campaign just a few months away, the United States was the clear victor in the Cold War. The nations of Eastern Europe that had been under the Soviet thumb had discarded communism, and the USSR did not try to stop them.

As president, George Bush scored a number of victories in foreign policy. After he took office in 1989, Bush met repeatedly with then Soviet president Mikhail Gorbachev to discuss the eventual end of the Cold War.

Finally, the failure of the Soviet Union's economy brought the collapse of communism on its home ground. The gigantic country began to break up, forming new states that moved toward democracy and capitalism.

The Bush administration took credit not only for Operation Desert Storm and the collapse of communism, but also for removing the Panamanian dictator Manuel Noriega from power in 1989 and arresting him on drug charges.

Trouble Brews for Bush

For his foreign policy, Bush was getting straight A's. But with the election looming ahead, these victories had a hollow ring. Even abroad, there were some problems. Iraq's Saddam Hussein was still in power. And critics raised questions about why the United States had treated him almost as a friend right up to his invasion of Kuwait.

President Bush's desire for free trade between countries was also creating political problems for him. Free trade meant letting imports compete freely with American goods. American workers, such as those who make cars, feared that this policy could cost them their jobs. In the spring of 1992, the president traveled to Japan to improve trade relations, but the trip appeared to be a failure. When he got sick at a banquet and threw up on the Japanese prime minister, the trip became the source of jokes the world over.

Oddly enough, some of President Bush's greatest triumphs created his biggest problems. The threat of global communism was one reason many people had voted Republican in 1988. For many years it seemed to the majority of Americans that the Republicans handled foreign affairs better than the Democrats. Without the foreign threat, the voters turned more toward domestic issues. And there, George Bush was in big trouble.

The economic expansion that had begun at the end of 1982 lasted for a number of years. People gave the Republicans credit for it, and that prosperity helped Bush

A Russian man tramples on a fallen statue of Yakov Sverdlov, the Communist leader who assassinated the Russian czar after the Bolshevik Revolution of 1917. In celebration of a move toward democracy, statues such as this were torn down all across the former Soviet Union after the collapse of communism in 1991.

By the fall of 1991, the United States was feeling the most serious effects of economic recession. Unemployment rose dramatically as businesses cut back to survive the tough economy.

win in 1988. But in 1990, not long before the beginnings of trouble in the Persian Gulf, the steam had gone out of the economy. Signs of decline were already appearing, but the war, and the few months of good feeling after it, helped to alleviate the downturn. By autumn 1991, however, the economy dipped more sharply and was clearly in a recession. Unemployment rose, and those with jobs began to fear that they might lose them.

As was the case in the 1980s, the U.S. government was spending more money than it took in, thus increasing the national debt. By 1990, Americans worried that future generations would have to make good on this debt. But when President Bush agreed to a slight increase in taxes in 1990 in an effort to deal with the problem, many of his supporters were furious. In the 1988 election campaign, George Bush had promised that there would be no new taxes. "Read my lips," he had said. "No new taxes." Now he had gone back on his word.

Bush had also said in 1988 that he would be both the "education president" and the "environmental president." But he had produced no new major education programs. And on the environment, he was fast making enemies. He signed the Clean Air Act of 1990, but when the recession hit, Bush favored business interests, which said that too many rules about air pollution would halt economic growth.

Controversy over air pollution pointed up a basic political problem for George Bush. Like the Democrats, the Republicans depended on the support of a combination of groups. For example, most Republicans wanted taxes kept low. But on an issue like the environment, Republicans differed. Some, for example, valued clean air over economic growth. This was also true of many independents who had voted for Reagan and Bush.

Another issue that split Republicans posed a bigger threat to Bush's reelection. It involved the treatment and rights of women.

In the fall of 1991, the Senate held hearings to confirm the president's nomination of Clarence Thomas to the Supreme Court. Anita Hill, who had worked in government with Thomas, claimed that he had harassed her with sexual comments. He denied it.

For several days, Americans watched the televised hearings. Who was telling the truth, Hill or Thomas? The testimony given could not provide the answer. But the treatment of Hill by Republican senators angered many women. The Republicans seemed to act as if Hill were on trial for lying.

The debate over abortion rights split Republicans even more. Part of Bush's support came from people who, on religious grounds, opposed abortion as murder. But many others who had voted Republican—especially middle-class voters in the suburbs and many women—felt that the government should not get involved in the issue. They said that women should make this choice themselves.

The national debate over abortion rights became a potent issue in the 1992 campaign. Democrat Bill Clinton declared himself to be pro-choice, while Republican George Bush renewed his loyalty to the causes of the pro-life movement.

Emotions were highly charged on both sides. In the final analysis, Bush opposed the right to have an abortion, making it likely that he would lose the vote of many women.

A Democratic Opportunity

When Operation Desert Storm ended, George Bush was riding high on a wave of American pride and patriotism. But by November 1991, he was a more inviting target for the Democrats. The effect of the weakening economy on Bush's chances showed up dramatically in the 1991 state and local elections.

Bush's former attorney general, Richard Thornburgh, was heavily favored to win the Senate seat in Pennsylvania. But he was defeated in an upset by the Democrat Harris Wofford, a former college president. Wofford attacked the president's economic policies. He made a special issue of the lack of medical insurance for many Americans and the high price of coverage for those who had it. And when he said, "It's time to take care of our own people, the middle class," he sounded a theme popular with voters.

Just as voters often viewed Republicans as having the more successful foreign policy, the Democrats were usually seen as stronger on domestic issues. The Democratic party had reduced unemployment and poverty and had pushed for laws like Medicare that helped the elderly. It was the party of Franklin Roosevelt's New Deal and Lyndon Johnson's Great Society. Democrats had also fought hardest for laws protecting civil rights.

Because of their stand on issues like these, the Democrats once seemed to have the presidency all but locked up. From 1932 to 1968, except for eight years in the 1950s, the White House had been theirs. Now, with Americans turning their attention again to problems at home, they had an excellent chance to regain the presidency in 1992.

A Democratic Dilemma

But the Democrats, like the Republicans, depended on a combination, or coalition, of voters. More so than the Republicans', the traditional Democratic coalition had fallen apart. Because of this, they had not won the presidency since 1976.

During the 1930s, President Roosevelt had combined working people, city dwellers, immigrants, farmers, southern whites, and blacks in the South and North into a strong coalition that lasted almost four decades. But changes in America undermined this group.

Unions, which had contributed campaign workers and money to the Democratic party, were in decline. Their

Franklin Delano Roosevelt (waving), who was president from 1933 to 1945, helped to create a new coalition of working people, urban dwellers, and farmers. This union formed the basis for America's modern Democratic party.

membership had been shrinking steadily. Also dropping was their influence. Democratic candidates were now careful of being seen as too much under the unions' sway.

Democratic support for civil rights angered southern whites. By the 1960s, many had gone over to the Republican party. Large corporate farms pushed out the owners of smaller spreads, also reducing a source of Democratic strength. Many children of the workers and immigrants in the cities got better educations and better-paying jobs than did their parents. This new generation moved to the suburbs, became more conservative, and began to vote Republican.

In both cities and suburbs, blacks and whites clashed over access to housing, jobs, and good schools. How could the Democratic party begin to unite them? On what measures to improve social welfare and strengthen the economy could it get these groups to agree? How could the party win back Democrats who had voted for Reagan and Bush?

The old Democratic policy of using big spending and big government to deal with big problems such as unemployment and poverty was no longer popular with the majority of voters. In the suburbs, where most voters lived, the last thing people appeared to want was higher taxes to pay for such programs.

Voters linked the Democrats with the growth of welfare. The party appeared too comfortable with having government take care of everything. Many thought Democrats weren't tough enough on crime. Others tied them to groups perceived by many as outside the mainstream, such as homosexuals. By 1970, for the first time since the 1930s, the Democrats were no longer named by a majority of Americans as their party.

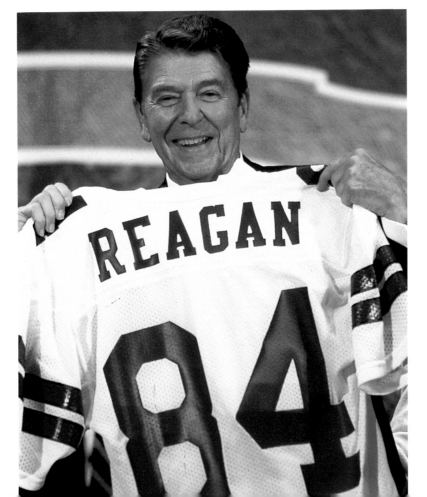

Ronald Reagan, who was president from 1980 to 1988, brought a new form of popular conservatism to the White House. George Bush, who was Reagan's vice president, rode the wave of Reagan's popularity when he ran for president in 1988.

Democrat Jimmy Carter had been elected president in 1976 largely because people were disgusted with Republican president Richard Nixon, who resigned in 1974 as a result of the Watergate scandal. But in 1980, Californian Ronald Reagan beat Carter by appealing to many Democrats and independents who felt that the Democratic party no longer reflected the proper ideals.

In 1984, Walter Mondale, who had been vice president under Carter, won the Democratic nomination. Mondale said that to reduce the budget deficit Americans would have to pay more taxes. He was buried in a landslide as Ronald Reagan won a second term.

In 1988, the Democrats nominated Massachusetts governor Michael Dukakis. He said the issue was "competence"—who could best manage the government. But Dukakis came off as colorless and not passionate about any issue. He did well only at the end of the campaign, when he returned to the old Democratic issues of jobs and social welfare. But by then it was too late.

Democratic Strategies

How could the Democrats overcome their problems? One possibility was to look south for a presidential candidate. That's what they had done the last time they won, in 1976, when they picked the moderate Georgia governor Jimmy Carter. Carter was a white southerner who was popular with black voters and with independents.

Tapping into discontent with President Bush's focus on foreign policy was also promising. George Mitchell, the Democratic majority leader in the Senate, said on March 4, 1991: "In the wake of the war, the president says he seeks a new world order. We say, join us in putting our own house in order. Our first priority must be the American people and economic growth and jobs in the United States."

Both parties had plenty of ammunition for bashing their opponents. For each problem the president blamed on an

Democrats used a somewhat new strategy when they ran Jimmy Carter for president in 1976. Carter, a relative unknown who was governor of Georgia, appealed to many southern Democrats and to those who mistrusted political "insiders" who had spent years in Washington.

uncooperative Democratic Congress, the Democrats came back with a problem that should have been addressed by the president. But many Americans were growing tired of listening to their leaders blame each other for the past. Unemployed, worried, and disillusioned, voters wanted hope for change more than anything else. Skeptical and angry about the political process, and generally disgusted by government scandals, broken promises, and verbal attacks on politicians, Americans cried out for a concrete plan that could address the real issues facing the nation. The most pressing problem was the economy, but other domestic issues such as national health care, crime, and education were badly in need of attention. The man who could best convince Americans of his ability to solve these problems would surely win the election of 1992.

Chapter 2

The Rules of the Game

How are people in America nominated for the office of president?

Although the Constitution says nothing about political parties, they have become the means by which we choose who will be on the ballot when we vote. Through most of America's history, there have been only two major parties. Since the Civil War, these parties have been the Democrats and the Republicans. In some years, especially when times are bad and voters are unhappy with the choices offered by these parties, many people have voted for independent candidates. But since 1860 only Republicans and Democrats have actually made it to the White House.

The way that each political party picks its candidate for president has changed greatly over the past twenty-five years. Delegates still gather at the Democratic and Republican national conventions during the summer before the election to decide who will run. But the party's delegates are chosen differently from the way they were chosen before the 1970s. Voters have gained a greater role, while party leaders play a smaller part.

Raising money to pay for the process has also changed and become more regulated in recent years. The funds

America's two major political parties have established a complex system for choosing their candidates.

Opposite:
Influence from powerful political bosses played a major role in the candidate-selection process in the early twentieth century. Here, at a typical voting booth in 1905, voting was done in front of others, and voters were frequently told which candidate should receive support.

The "Smoke-Filled Room"

Before the 1970s, local and state political leaders played the biggest role in deciding whom to nominate for president. The voters had little direct say in the matter. Big-city mayors, like the Democrats' Richard Daley of Chicago, and governors, such as New York Republican Nelson Rockefeller, had enormous influence. State parties actually chose the delegates to the national conventions. But men like Daley and Rockefeller controlled the state parties.

These politicians were powerful because they and people who worked under them could offer party workers jobs and favors. People who wanted to run for higher office had to get the support of these and other political "bosses." They did this by forming alliances of state and local politicians. Much of this dealing went on behind closed doors. Many old-time political bosses were cigar smokers. So these deals were said to take place in "smoke-filled rooms."

Was this system entirely bad? Some observers don't think so. Because candidates weren't chosen until the convention, anything that happened before the convention affected the nomination. Today, victories in early primaries sometimes produce a heavy favorite by March. If, for any reason, people afterward have doubts about such a candidate, it may be too late for anyone else to enter the race. Some Democrats who were unhappy with Bill Clinton felt this way in late spring of 1992. But, by then, Clinton had the nomination locked up.

Often politicians know best who can win the fall general election. Today, the focus is on who can score quick victories in a few early primaries, where the voters may not represent the feelings of most Americans. Such victories are empty if they produce nominees who eventually go on to lose in the national election in November.

used to come primarily from private sources and from the candidates themselves. Today, the federal government pays for much of the campaign with money raised through taxes. It also regulates private fund-raising. This new role for the government applies to the general election in the fall as well as to the contest for each party's nomination.

Choosing the Candidates

We've come a long way since party professionals picked the candidates in "smoke-filled rooms." Today, the contests for the nominations are more open—and cost much more money.

Methods of nominating presidential candidates started to change ninety years ago. At the turn of the century, a spirit of reform swept America. Voters felt they should have more control over their government. Many states passed laws that said that before the general election took place, each party had to hold separate state elections, called "primaries," to choose its candidate. All those registered in a party could vote, as they did in November. But this time they would be picking delegates to the conventions who would then pick the person to run for president. The people, not the politicians, would choose.

Over the years, however, interest in these primaries declined. Many states went back to having the party professionals make the final selection. But by the 1960s, primaries came back into favor. Gradually, more states passed laws requiring the use of primaries to choose delegates to the national convention. By 1992, thirty-seven states had these laws.

Who gets to vote in the primaries? Most states allow only people registered in a party to vote in that party's primary. But a few states let voters cast their ballot in either party's contest. These are called "open primaries."

The federal government also plays a role in deciding who can vote. In party primaries, as in the general election, it's against the law to prevent someone from voting because of his or her race or sex. The Twenty-sixth Amendment to the Constitution, which lowered the voting age from twenty-one to eighteen, also applies here.

How many delegates to the national nominating convention are at stake in each state primary? The parties decide. They consider the state's population and how well the party has done in that state in recent elections.

A candidate who wins a state's primary does not usually get all the delegates from that state. All candidates who win a certain minimum number of votes get some delegates. The number is usually in proportion to the total number of votes he or she received in the primary.

Only in the California Republican primary does the candidate who gets the most votes get all the state's delegates. This "winner-take-all" rule is forbidden by the Democratic party.

Non-primary states choose delegates through "caucuses," which are local meetings of the party held at a specific time and place. Everyone registered in the party holding the caucus can attend and vote for delegates. These delegates then go to a state convention where they, in turn, choose delegates to the national nominating convention. The voter turnout in states having caucuses is usually even smaller than the 25 percent of all eligible voters who cast their ballots in primaries.

National parties have a say not only in how state delegates to the national convention are chosen, but in who they are. In recent years, the Democratic party has required each state to have an equal number of male and female delegates and a fair number of minorities. The national Republican party only suggests that state parties keep these factors in mind when naming delegates. Candidates choose the specific people to become delegates.

In the Democratic party, 10 percent of all delegates to the national nominating convention are not chosen by voters. These "super delegates" are Democratic members of Congress, governors, and party officials. They have a say because they are thought to know what it takes to win a national election. Also, from experience, they might know what kind of person could actually do the best job as president.

Dates with Destiny

When primaries and caucuses are held is an important part of the process. They begin in February of the presidential election year with the Iowa caucuses and end in June with the California primary. The date on which delegates are chosen can affect the race in both parties. Early victories, even in a few small states, such as New Hampshire, can give people the feeling that the candidate who is winning has become the favorite. In fact, little New Hampshire's primary, which is the first, gets much more attention than others simply because it is the first.

Southerners in the Democratic party, who tend to be conservative, felt that this was unfair. Liberals could focus

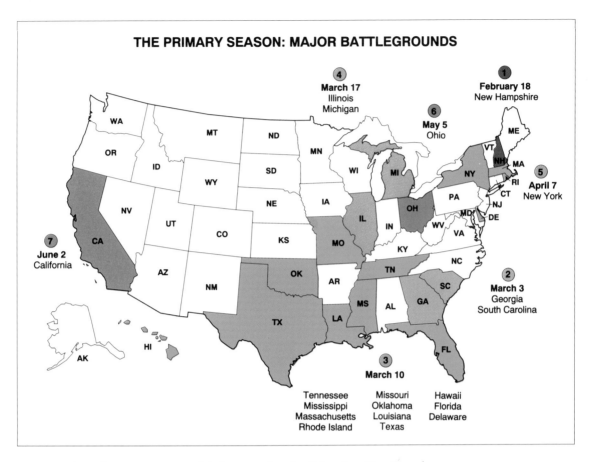

THE PRIMARY SEASON: MAJOR BATTLEGROUNDS

4
March 17
Illinois
Michigan

1
February 18
New Hampshire

6
May 5
Ohio

5
April 7
New York

7
June 2
California

2
March 3
Georgia
South Carolina

3
March 10

Tennessee	Missouri	Hawaii
Mississippi	Oklahoma	Florida
Massachusetts	Louisiana	Delaware
Rhode Island	Texas	

on the first few contests, which were in the North. By the time the South voted, a liberal might seem more popular than he or she really was in the country as a whole.

To stop this, Democratic-controlled state legislatures in the South moved up their primaries. Six of them are now held in March, on a day known as "Super Tuesday" because so much is at stake on that day. This gives the South more of a say in who will be nominated.

Another Way to Get on the Ballot

There is a way of getting around the whole system of primaries and caucuses. A person can get on the ballot in any state by having a certain number of registered voters sign a petition. Each state has laws that say how this must be done and how many signatures are needed. In 1992, in fact, one candidate started down this independent path to the White House.

Paying for It

More primaries mean more campaigns. Candidates must travel more and spend more on television commercials, office supplies, salaries, computers, telephones, and everything else needed in a campaign.

The general election in November has also become more expensive in recent years. Television commercials have evolved into the most important and effective way to reach voters. And television time is very costly.

Where does all this money come from?

It used to be up to the parties and the candidates themselves to raise it. But in 1971, Congress began to limit how much could be collected from private contributors and how much could be spent. It also said that candidates had to keep careful records and report where their money came from.

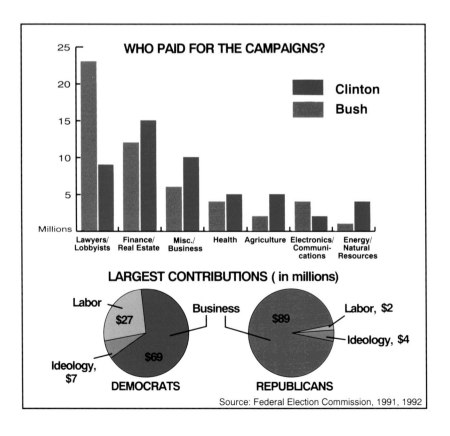

Source: Federal Election Commission, 1991, 1992

The government now sets aside a specific amount of public funds, raised from taxes, which all candidates receive. To qualify for these "matching funds," candidates have to get a certain number of votes in the primaries. In addition, they must raise specific amounts of money on their own. The government also pays for the national nominating conventions and helps to pay for the final campaign in the fall.

Laws now limit the amount of money that individuals can give to a candidate in either a primary or the general election. Large groups, such as corporations and unions, can also give money by forming Political Action Committees, or PACs. Individuals interested in a particular issue, such as the environment, can band together in PACs, too. In either case, all of the direct contributions to candidates are limited and must be reported.

These regulations are not airtight. One way around them is to contribute to state Democratic and Republican parties for their general expenses. These contributions have no limits. This so-called "soft money" can pay for phone calls, pamphlets, getting out the vote on Election Day, or any other vague or discretionary expense.

In fact, general-expense contributions help presidential candidates. What the state parties would have spent on these general expenses can now go toward their presidential candidate's campaign.

There's a Catch

There's one big problem with the public funding of elections. The rules about matching funds and spending limits apply only to those who accept money from the government to help pay for their campaigns. What about someone rich enough to pay for it out of his or her own pocket, turning down any government help and avoiding spending limitations? There are a number of people in the United States who could afford it. In 1992, one of them decided to run for president.

Chapter 3

The Primaries: Off and Running

There is never a lack of candidates for one of the most powerful positions in the world.

In the fall of 1991, several Democrats declared that they would run for president. The front-runner was Arkansas governor Bill Clinton, a moderate. He said America could better solve its social problems by supporting economic growth than by spending money on welfare.

Clinton, 46 years old, had won a Rhodes Scholarship to study at Oxford University in England after he attended the University of Arkansas. He was attorney general of Arkansas from 1977 to 1979 and governor of the state from 1979 to 1981. After losing a race for reelection, partly because voters felt he was too removed from the people, he moderated his politics and changed his governing style. He was elected governor again in 1983 and held that position throughout the race for president.

Senator Bob Kerrey of Nebraska also entered the race. He stressed the need for national health care. Senator Tom Harkin, who wanted more government programs to help people, said he would run, too.

Former Massachusetts senator Paul Tsongas, who had survived a bout with cancer, also "threw his hat into the ring." Tsongas wanted government to do more to help

> "This has been a tough, weird political year," President Bush said in June.

Opposite:
Former Massachussetts senator Paul Tsongas got off to a strong start during the 1992 primary season. After only months of campaigning, however, Tsongas ran out of money and withdrew from the contest.

Where Were the Democratic Leaders?

As the candidates for the Democratic nomination entered the contest in 1992, some people seemed to be missing. None of the party's most prominent leaders were joining the race.

Massachusetts senator Ted Kennedy had been the liberal spokesperson for the Democrats for almost two decades. But questions about his personal life had arisen since 1969. He was involved then in an auto accident at Chappaquiddick on Martha's Vineyard. A young woman drowned in that accident. In

Jesse Jackson became an influential national leader during his bid for the presidency in 1988.

1991, Kennedy's nephew William Smith was accused of rape, and his uncle testified at his trial. The verdict was "not guilty," but people were reminded of the senator's past problems.

Jesse Jackson won several contests in the race for the 1988 presidential nomination. A prominent African-American leader, he had rallied many whites as well as blacks to his cause in a "Rainbow Coalition." In 1990 Jackson was elected representative of the District of Columbia. He also hosted a television show. But he declined to run for president in 1992.

New Jersey senator Bill Bradley, a former basketball player, was also considered "presidential material." But his support for higher taxes angered voters, and he barely won reelection to the Senate in the fall of 1990.

Virginia's governor Douglas Wilder and Senator Charles Robb were both popular. Each was thinking of running. However, a feud between them and charges of scandal against Robb and "dirty tricks" by his staff weakened both men.

Polls showed that Governor Mario Cuomo of New York would be a very popular candidate with independents as well as Democrats. For a few weeks in the fall of 1991, it looked as if he might run. Cuomo teased reporters, hinting one day that he would get into the race, the next speaking as if he wouldn't. Finally, in December, he gave a definite no. He said that he couldn't run, because he had to devote all his time to his state's budget.

business. Former California governor Jerry Brown entered as a reform candidate. Brown attacked corruption and the role that big money played in politics. Brown also wanted more protection for the environment.

On the Republican side, President Bush received an unpleasant surprise. Just when he thought his nomination would be a sure thing, conservative television commentator Patrick Buchanan decided to challenge the president. Buchanan was given no chance of winning, but his sharp criticisms of Bush and the current administration made many voters take notice.

By February, all eyes were on New Hampshire, the site of the first primary. In 1992, as in most years, New Hampshire voters ignored the early favorites and the experts' forecasts. By the time New Hampshire citizens voted, they had the front-runners scrambling to maintain their positions.

The Republicans: Bush Beats Buchanan

George Bush did not formally enter the race until February 12, only a week before the New Hampshire primary. Buchanan had campaigned for weeks up and down the state, meeting people face-to-face and listening to their fears about losing their jobs. He also shared their anger about the president's broken promise not to raise taxes.

Buchanan tapped into many resentments that Americans were feeling. His ads suggested that racial quotas hurt whites by favoring minorities for jobs. He also said that too many immigrants were entering the country and were competing with native-born Americans for work. Buchanan warned that free trade, supported by Bush, would also mean a loss of jobs because cheaper foreign goods would put American firms out of business. He called for America to pay less attention to foreign affairs and to devote more energy to problems at home.

George Bush and Dan Quayle officially kicked off their reelection campaign in Washington on February 12, 1992. With them were their wives, Barbara Bush and Marilyn Quayle.

Conservative political commentator Patrick Buchanan challenged President Bush for the Republican nomination in 1992. Although never a serious threat, Buchanan did receive significant support from Republicans during the primaries.

Bush apologized for breaking his "no new taxes" pledge. His television ads showed him in the Oval Office, stressing his experience. Bush did not even mention Buchanan's name.

Bush won the February 18 primary. But Buchanan got 37 percent of the vote, a very high total for a candidate running against an incumbent president. The White House had reason for concern. No one thought that Bush would lose the Republican nomination. But party leaders began to fear that a strong Democratic challenge might beat their man in the fall.

In the next few primaries, Buchanan continued to pick up 20 to 30 percent of the votes, showing that many Republicans were unhappy with their president. But even with his surprisingly good showings in the early primaries, Buchanan began to fade. Television and newspapers gave him increasingly less attention. His campaign contributions dried up, and his vote totals dropped. Well before the final primaries, President Bush's renomination was assured.

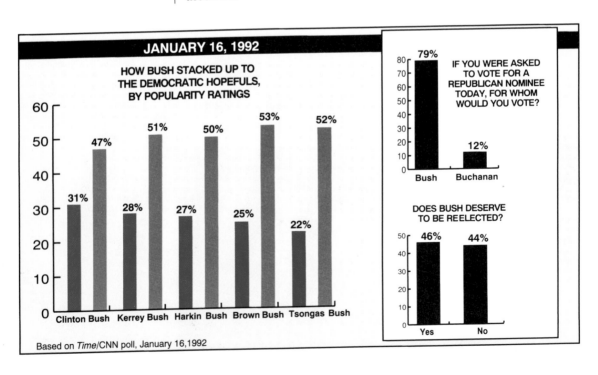

JANUARY 16, 1992

HOW BUSH STACKED UP TO THE DEMOCRATIC HOPEFULS, BY POPULARITY RATINGS

Clinton 31% Bush 47%	Kerrey 28% Bush 51%	Harkin 27% Bush 50%	Brown 25% Bush 53%	Tsongas 22% Bush 52%

IF YOU WERE ASKED TO VOTE FOR A REPUBLICAN NOMINEE TODAY, FOR WHOM WOULD YOU VOTE?

Bush 79% Buchanan 12%

DOES BUSH DESERVE TO BE REELECTED?

Yes 46% No 44%

Based on *Time*/CNN poll, January 16, 1992

On the Democratic Side

Like Bush on the Republican side, Bill Clinton, the early Democratic favorite, was not having an easy time of it, especially when a supermarket tabloid reported that the Arkansas governor had carried on a secret twelve-year romance with a woman named Gennifer Flowers. This was only the first of several questions raised about the candidate's "character" over the next several weeks. Clinton said that there had been some problems in his marriage. But he also complained that the press wanted only to dredge up scandal, while he wanted to talk about the issues.

New charges continued to surface, keeping the focus on Clinton's personal life. Did the Arkansas governor unfairly avoid military service during the Vietnam War? Did he once smoke marijuana? Did he inhale it?

Paul Tsongas, from Massachusetts, gained the most when Clinton stumbled in New Hampshire. Tsongas said that what Americans needed was "hard work and sacrifice." He traveled the state, handing out a book about his policies, *A Call to Economic Arms*. With a name already familiar to New Hampshire's voters, Tsongas gained rapidly on Clinton.

Tsongas won the primary with just over 30 percent of the vote, with Clinton several points behind and the rest of the candidates farther back.

Two weeks later, on March 3, Clinton won the primary in Georgia, a southern state, where everyone expected the man from Arkansas to do well. But Tsongas won in Maryland.

Kerrey and Harkin, after winning only a few delegates and with funds running low, dropped out of the race in early March. The field was now down to Clinton, Tsongas, and Brown. And Super Tuesday loomed ahead.

Being a southerner, Clinton had the advantage on March 10. Tsongas won in his home state of Massachusetts and in neighboring Rhode Island. But Clinton took the

Bill Clinton officially began his primary campaign efforts in New Hampshire in January 1992.

Nebraska senator Bob Kerrey entered the race for the Democratic nomination on a platform that stressed the need for nationalized health care. Although his ideas won favor, his campaign did not survive the first few primary contests.

Senator Tom Harkin went into the Democratic primaries with a strong confidence boost from the Iowa caucuses. His showing in the primaries, however, was not enough to sustain his candidacy.

other nine contests, including the delegate-rich states of Texas and Florida. Florida was the key, because Tsongas was thought to have a chance to win there. Victory would have shown his appeal outside his own section of the country, making him a more serious candidate for the Democratic nomination.

Brown trailed badly almost everywhere in the nation, but a few of his key messages did seem to resonate with many Americans. Young voters favored Brown's strong policies on the environment, and union workers liked his anti-big-business ideas about government. To make a strong statement against corruption and unfair political influence on candidates by the wealthy, Brown established a national toll-free number to accept campaign contributions. The donations, however, could not exceed $100 per caller.

After the primaries on March 17 went to Clinton, Paul Tsongas, whose campaign had looked so promising after

New Hampshire only a few weeks earlier, was now out of money. On March 19, he announced that he was also out of the race.

The April New York primary suddenly became a show-down between Clinton and Brown. After almost ignoring Brown for weeks as a minor candidate, the media had started to pay attention when Brown squeaked by Clinton in Connecticut by 1 percent. Debate raged over his plan to replace the income tax with a flat, universal tax of 13 percent. Whom would it benefit, the poor or the rich?

There was not great enthusiasm for either man in New York. On the morning of the primary, *The New York Times* summed up the feelings of many voters: "Brown seems weird and a little slick, Clinton slick and a little weird."

When Clinton won in New York and Brown finished third to Tsongas, a "ghost candidate" whose name was still on the ballot despite his withdrawal, the former California governor lost the spotlight. Brown's coverage by

Jerry Brown entered the Democratic race with an anti-big-business message about government that appealed to many young voters. He also established a national toll-free number to accept campaign contributions, each of which could not exceed $100.

the media decreased sharply. But the attention devoted to Clinton's flaws continued. Polls showed that voters were wary of him. On April 20, *Time* magazine's cover story was "Why Voters Don't Trust Clinton."

There was much talk of a "stop Clinton" movement. Some politicians hoped to keep him short of the votes needed for nomination, forcing the July convention to take more than one ballot. Then, they hoped, back-room bargaining could produce a new, stronger compromise candidate.

How Much Do We Need to Know About a Candidate?

Is the private life of the person we pick for the presidency that important? Does it tell us how he or she will act in office? Has the media gone too far in uncovering everything about the people who want to occupy the White House?

These questions have arisen in elections for many years. They came up in 1992 when Bill Clinton ran in the primaries. It was not the first time scandalous information had surfaced about a candidate. In 1884, Republicans made much of the fact that Democrat Grover Cleveland, a bachelor, had fathered a child. Despite this ploy, Cleveland won two presidential elections.

One hundred years later, in 1984, when Democratic senator Gary Hart of Colorado was campaigning during the primaries, the press revealed his romantic activities with a woman named Donna Rice. Hart was considered one of the most able politicians in his party at the time of the scandal. Nevertheless, Hart's campaign came to a screeching halt as soon as news of his private life became public.

Some people feel that "improper" behavior reveals important flaws in a person's character. They believe infidelity or similar actions suggest an inability to be the kind of leader the nation needs. That kind of person, they say, would also set a bad example for young people.

But others point out that Presidents Franklin Roosevelt, Dwight Eisenhower, and John Kennedy all had romances outside their marriages. These affairs, some say, did not seem to influence the kind of presidents these men became.

Nationwide publication of the photograph of Gary Hart and Donna Rice (below right) abruptly ended Hart's bid for the presidency in 1984.

Scandals plagued Clinton's early campaign. In January, Gennifer Flowers publicly announced that she had had a long-standing affair with Clinton.

But Clinton's well-organized campaign managed to keep churning out the victories, despite all the criticism. Paul Tsongas, urged by supporters to jump back into the race, decided against it. And when Clinton beat Brown by a two-to-one margin in Pennsylvania on April 28, the opposition to the Arkansas governor within the party started to melt. Super delegates, many of whom had been holding back, now began to jump on the Clinton bandwagon.

Clinton's victories in California and New Jersey on June 6 put him over the top. They won him enough delegates to assure his nomination.

A "Weird" Year

Ordinarily, politics in a presidential election year quiet down after the last primary. Then they flare up at the conventions. And they really get going when the fall campaign begins around Labor Day.

But this was not the scenario in 1992. "This has been a tough, weird political year," President Bush said in June. He said this partly because by then, the two-man race had suddenly acquired an extra man.

A Man Named Perot

While many voters preferred either Bush or Clinton, many others still felt that they were not getting a real choice. According to polls, as much as a third of the electorate felt this way.

Now one man offered himself as a different kind of choice. He talked straight, didn't look like a politician, and had a reputation for getting things done. He very quickly became a serious threat to the candidates of both major parties. His name was H. Ross Perot.

Who was this man? Perot, a Texan, had an all-American boyhood. His father taught him how to tame wild horses. He was an Eagle Scout with his own paper route. For college, he went to the U.S. Naval Academy.

The success of Electronic Data Systems (EDS), the company Perot founded in the 1960s, made him one of the richest men in America. It was a computer company that, among other things, helped states take care of health-insurance claims.

General Motors (GM) bought EDS in 1984, making Perot a member of the GM board of directors. The Texan complained that the executives at the huge auto company were too stuffy, too slow to change, and too out of touch with both their workers and their customers. (That was just the kind of thing that many voters were saying in 1992 about their political leaders.) Perot was forced out of GM. But he was becoming known as the "little guy" who would stand up to the "big guys."

As Perot prospered, he turned to public affairs. He worked for educational reform in Texas and volunteered to help the U.S. government look into the possibility that American soldiers were still being held in Vietnam.

On February 20, Perot appeared on the "Larry King Live" television show. On that show, the two men discussed the possibility of Perot running for president. Perot said he would do it if supporters got his name on

APRIL 6, 1992

IF THE ELECTION WERE HELD TODAY, WHOM WOULD YOU VOTE FOR?

Based on *Time* poll, April 5–6, 1992

In February, Ross Perot announced on a cable television talk show that he would run for president if his supporters got him on the ballot in all fifty states. His announcement set off a "grass-roots" campaign that spread rapidly; his information hot line got over a million calls during the second half of March.

the ballot in all fifty states. He also said he would put more than $100 million of his own money—which was estimated at $2.5 to 3.5 billion—behind the effort.

Perot's candidacy caught on quickly. A Perot information phone number got over one million calls in the second half of March. This candidate appealed to both liberals and conservatives. He did this despite his failure to be specific on the issues. When reporters asked him where he stood on problems such as health care, taxes, and the environment, he said he would consult the experts or hold nationwide "town meetings" through television to ask the people what they wanted done. Although his

The Other Option: Third-Party Candidates

Alabama governor George Wallace ran for president as an independent candidate in 1968. Wallace received 13.5 percent of the vote, more than any other independent candidate before 1992.

Just as the Constitution says nothing about political parties, there's no law in politics that says there must be only Democrats and Republicans. In fact, several times in our past, other parties have sprung up to challenge the two leading parties.

Most of the time, the two-party system works. It represents people with widely different views on the issues, while keeping the country stable. Partly as a result, America has not had a revolution or civil war for well over a hundred years.

The two-party system usually works because both parties are coalitions—groups having enough in common to join under one banner. Since there are always some conflicts between these groups, compromise is necessary. Each gives up a little to give the party wide enough appeal to win an election.

But what if the groups that make up a party can't compromise? In the 1850s, this happened with the problem of slavery. Many northern Democrats who opposed slavery could no longer go along with south-

positions were muddy, his message was clear. Perot presented himself as the feisty businessman who could make the tough decisions America needed to get its economy back on track. As a Washington outsider, Perot was a renegade symbol, a man who owed nothing to powerful interest groups and whose only obligation was "to the people" of the nation.

ern Democrats, who supported it. The other major party, the Whigs, couldn't come up with a policy on slavery that satisfied enough of its members. As a result, people breaking away from both parties plus independents formed a third party: the Republicans. They elected Abraham Lincoln, who soon found himself plagued with a civil war. After the war, the Republicans put together a stable coalition. They replaced the Whigs as the second major party.

Since then, third parties have played a role in national politics several times. In the 1890s, farmers hit by hard times felt that neither Republicans nor Democrats were listening to them. So they formed the Populist party, but the return of prosperity blunted its appeal.

In 1912, Theodore Roosevelt, who had already served as a Republican president, was considered too conservative by the Republican candidate, William Howard Taft. Roosevelt ran on the Progressive, or "Bull Moose," ticket. He drew enough Republican votes away from Taft to help ensure the election of the Democrat, Woodrow Wilson.

In more recent times, Alabama governor George Wallace's independent runs for president changed both major parties. He took advantage of the issue of race, which was splitting the Democrats. Many southern whites, union members, and suburbanites were unhappy with Democratic liberalism. They blamed rising crime, urban riots, and higher taxes on government policies that, they felt, favored blacks.

Wallace received 9.9 million votes in the 1968 election, most of which would have gone to Hubert Humphrey, the Democratic candidate. Humphrey lost a close race to Richard Nixon. In the solid South, so-called because it had been safe for Democratic candidates since the Civil War, the Republicans made big gains. As a result, the Republican party became strong in the South. And the Democrats were eventually forced to move away from liberalism.

In 1980, Congressman John Anderson, who had been a Republican, ran as an independent against President Carter and Ronald Reagan. Anderson strongly supported women's rights and was pro-environment, but he was conservative on economics. In many ways his politics were like those of Paul Tsongas. During the campaign, polls showed Anderson with the support of close to 15 percent of the voters. But on Election Day, many people seemed to think that a vote for him would be "thrown away" because he couldn't win. He finished with only about 7 percent of the popular vote, but helped reinstate the idea of an independent party that could effectively speak to many Americans.

Theodore Roosevelt

People didn't know where Perot stood on the issues, but they knew they liked him. One college student interviewed in April said: "He's not a politician. I feel like he's almost a human being."

By the end of May, some polls showed Perot leading Bush, with Clinton third. In state after state, Perot's followers got many more than the required number of

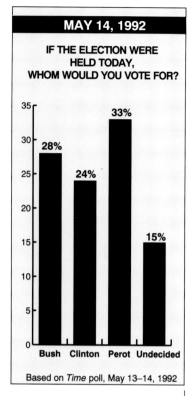

MAY 14, 1992

IF THE ELECTION WERE
HELD TODAY,
WHOM WOULD YOU VOTE FOR?

Bush 28%
Clinton 24%
Perot 33%
Undecided 15%

Based on *Time* poll, May 13–14, 1992

signatures to have his name added to the presidential ballot in November. No third-party candidate in history had ever looked so good at this stage of the race. But the campaign was far from over.

Just as the spotlight of national attention had focused on Bill Clinton's past, Perot's background came under scrutiny as soon as he stole the media spotlight. And the man from Texas did not like it.

Old charges that Perot's company, EDS, had billed state governments too much for services came up again. There were reports that Perot could work with others only when he got his own way completely. There were also claims that Perot's family had unfairly profited on certain Texas land deals.

Other gaffes followed. When asked if he would allow homosexuals in his cabinet, Perot didn't give a straight answer. Then he referred to a black audience as "you people" and had to apologize when many found this insulting. Although claiming to be outside politics, running a people's campaign, Perot hired professional political advisers. Gradually, he was getting a taste of what running for president was really like.

By mid-July, his standing in the polls began to dip. Although running hard, he had not yet formally announced his candidacy. Would the bubble burst?

Riots in Los Angeles

Race and poverty, major political issues in the campaigns of the 1960s, had moved into the background as America turned conservative in the 1970s and 1980s. But suddenly in 1992, race and poverty issues got everyone's attention.

On April 29, a California jury acquitted four white Los Angeles police officers on most of the charges related to beating a black man named Rodney King. Several days of rioting followed, in which more than fifty people died and millions of dollars worth of property was destroyed. It was the worst urban rioting since the 1960s.

President Bush blamed the rioting on liberal, Democratic social-welfare programs enacted in the 1960s and 1970s. He said the emphasis should not be on welfare but on encouraging business to invest in ghetto areas, thereby creating jobs.

On May 19, Vice President Dan Quayle seemed to put the blame on America's declining sense of morals. He cited the television show "Murphy Brown," in which the main character, although unmarried, had a baby. Quayle said that a "cultural elite" cheered the decline of "family values." This, Quayle asserted, had helped to bring on the riots. Considered a political liability to the Bush administration, Quayle had been under great pressure to resign. As part of an effort to "take charge" and lead a fight for a cause, Quayle was given the job of courting his party's conservative elements. Soon the message about America's eroding "family values" became Quayle's rallying cry. He spoke about it in all his speeches and cited it as a cause for most of the nation's serious problems. His speech about the Los Angeles riots was no different.

Clinton said the Los Angeles riots were the result of "twelve years of denial and neglect" by Republicans. People should have a bigger role in policing their own neighborhoods, he said. Clinton linked welfare to job training and called for the building of more public works, such as roads and bridges.

Ross Perot said the solution was "education, education, education."

Many voters still felt that none of the candidates was getting serious enough about the nation's problems. A Pittsburgh teacher said: "It's so frustrating. It's beyond anger. Bush, Clinton, they're the same. They're politicians. Let's get going, for God's sake. If it's more money for housing, fine. If it's tax cuts, fine. If it's tax increases, fine. Something, anything."

Dan Quayle sparked great controversy with his national speeches about a "cultural elite" in Hollywood that threatened "family values" in America. The most controversial of Quayle's speeches criticized television character Murphy Brown for having a baby as a single mother.

Chapter 4

The Conventions

The delegates wear funny hats, blow horns, wave signs, and cheer wildly. At times, the noise and commotion can be chaotic.

Political conventions have always been a little like New Year's Eve, the Fourth of July, and a baseball game combined. Today, because of the primaries, voters are likely to have chosen the nominee before the delegates meet. This was true for both parties in 1992. But even if some of the voting drama is gone, the "color" is still there.

Television covers each national convention for four nights. For the candidates the coverage is precious, free publicity. (There were 15,000 reporters covering the activities of the 5,000 delegates at the Democrats' convention.) Usually this kind of attention gives a candidate a boost in the polls. The increase he or she gets is called the "bounce."

Picking a Running Mate

Presidential candidates usually announce their choice for a running mate just before the convention. The delegates always approve the selection, no matter what.

Vice-presidential candidates are usually chosen in order to gain certain political advantages. They often come

New York City and Houston hosted America's grandest political shows in 1992.

Opposite:
A Democratic delegate enjoys the fanfare of the national convention in New York City in July 1992.

The favorable press coverage of this trip, and Perot's withdrawal, sent Clinton's standing in the polls soaring. He was leading President Bush by about 20 percent.

The President in Hot Water

Meanwhile, George Bush was in big trouble. He was down in the polls, his advisers disagreed about what to do, and his vice president was coming under attack. Many

The Democratic National Convention: New York City, July 1992

The Democratic national convention opened on July 13, 1992. During the course of the gathering, the Democrats stressed the need for change in American government and criticized President Bush for the failing economy. *Top*: Clinton and Gore show their solidarity. *Left*: A delegate holds a sign that expresses the need for national health care, one of the core issues in the campaign. *Opposite*: Delegates listen to speeches (*inset*) and then celebrate the formal nomination and acceptance of Bill Clinton and Al Gore as the Democratic presidential and vice-presidential candidates.

Republican politicians were saying that Dan Quayle should withdraw because his unpopularity would pull the president down. Some even felt that Bush himself was the problem and that he should step aside.

Moderate Republicans were unhappy with conservative control of their party. Americans were most worried about the economy, said the polls, but conservative Republicans wanted to talk about "family values" only.

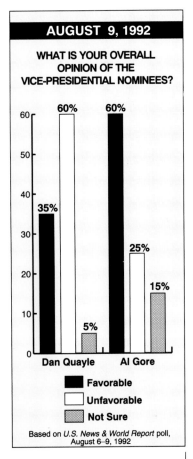

AUGUST 9, 1992

WHAT IS YOUR OVERALL
OPINION OF THE
VICE-PRESIDENTIAL NOMINEES?

■ Favorable
□ Unfavorable
▨ Not Sure

Based on *U.S. News & World Report* poll,
August 6–9, 1992

Abortion was an especially difficult problem. The Republican platform called for a complete ban on it, but many Republicans strongly disagreed with their party. Even more feared that this stance would offend women voters and would badly hurt the party in the election.

Abortion took even more of the spotlight when both President Bush and Vice President Quayle seemed to waver on the issue. Reporters asked each what he would do if his daughter or granddaughter told him that she was pregnant and wanted to have an abortion. Both said that they would support her decision. Were they, then, backing the pro-choice position? Or were they saying abortion was all right for their loved ones but not for everyone else? Or were they perhaps trying to have it both ways—have the platform please the conservatives, while their comments satisfied the moderates? Barbara Bush, the president's wife, went so far as to say that the abortion issue did not belong in the Republican platform at all.

The Republicans Gather in Houston

Many moderate Republican officeholders stayed away from their convention. With conservatives in charge, they felt that they didn't belong there. And the tone of much of the convention, which opened in the Houston Astrodome on August 17, reflected the moderates' fears.

Archconservatives Pat Buchanan, the man Bush had defeated in the primaries, and evangelist Pat Robertson made fiery prime-time speeches at the convention. They were critical of homosexuality, tough on those who had AIDS, and seemed to suggest that feminism and equality for women were taking America in the wrong direction.

Ronald Reagan, former president and leader of the modern conservative movement, also spoke. Republican leaders hoped that the affection many voters still held for Reagan would rub off on George Bush. Marilyn Quayle told the convention she was proud to have given up her career as a lawyer in order to stay home and raise her children. (This was meant to suggest criticism of Hillary Clinton, Bill Clinton's wife, who was also a lawyer but did not give up her work.) Barbara Bush, more popular in the polls than any candidate, also addressed the delegates.

In his acceptance speech, President Bush took credit for the "death of communism" around the world. He also hit hard at Clinton. He criticized the Arkansas governor for his inexperience in foreign affairs and questioned his character. What was the governor doing while the president had to make the hard decisions about Operation Desert Storm? he asked. Bush said, "While I bit the bullet, he bit his nails."

Bush charged that Clinton was really a liberal who would raise taxes. The president promised to cut taxes if reelected. He said he was wrong to have signed the 1990 tax-increase bill, but blamed it on the Democratic Congress. He attacked Congress for setting up a "roadblock" to the change the president wanted to bring about.

Although the Republican convention put George Bush and his party in the spotlight for four days, the candidates did not receive the traditional "bounce" common to postconvention weeks. The national coverage helped only marginally to boost Bush for a few days, but it was a short-lived rise. Many political analysts felt that the realities of a poor economy were affecting so many in such a serious way that few Americans remained optimistic for more than a day or two past the convention.

Bush quickly realized just how tough his fight would have to be. He had essentially lost all of the political advantages an incumbent usually has when running for reelection. Suddenly, being the president was more of a political hindrance than a help. Following his strategy from the 1988 election, where he also trailed in the polls for much of the campaign, Bush brought Secretary of State James Baker back to the White House to run the reelection campaign. Many people in Washington and

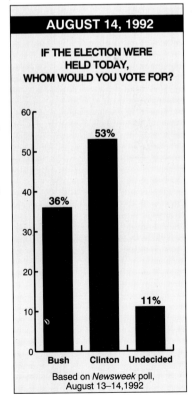

AUGUST 14, 1992

IF THE ELECTION WERE HELD TODAY, WHOM WOULD YOU VOTE FOR?

Bush 36%
Clinton 53%
Undecided 11%

Based on *Newsweek* poll, August 13–14, 1992

the rest of the country criticized the president for playing
"fast and loose" with the nation's most important posts.
But the president felt that he had no choice. Americans all
across the country were reeling from the effects of unemployment and a weak economy. Voter anger toward the
White House was much more noticeable than it had ever

The Republican National Convention: Houston, Texas, August 1992

The Republican convention opened in the Houston Astrodome on August 17, 1992. During the course of the convention, Republicans highlighted the many gains America had made in the areas of foreign policy and criticized Bill Clinton and the Democratic Congress for leading the country toward more "tax and spend" policies. *Left*: Barbara Bush—whose popularity peaked during the convention—delivered a key speech to the delegates. *Below*: The Bushes and the Quayles celebrate the adulation of their party's delegates on the last night of the convention. *Opposite*: Conventioneers revel in the festive atmosphere of the Astrodome.

been before. Both the Clinton campaign and the Perot campaign had hammered home to the American people the need for change in the government, and it seemed to work. By the beginning of September, George Bush clearly knew that he was about to spend the next two months fighting for his political life.

UNITED WE
STAND,
AMERICA

52

The Final Stretch

What else could happen in this strange election year? Early in October, Americans found out. Just when Bush and Clinton were settling into a two-man race, Ross Perot was heard from again.

Perot said neither candidate was seriously confronting the most important issue: balancing the budget. On October 1, he reentered the race, officially, this time. He named as his running mate Vice Admiral James B. Stockdale, a former prisoner of war in Vietnam.

If Ross Perot expected that he could pick up just where he had left off in July, he was mistaken. The man who had once actually led in some polls started his second effort with no more than 10 percent of the potential votes. It even looked to some as if his reentry might have little effect on the main battle, which now loomed between Bush and Clinton.

Election Day was still a month away, and Ross Perot was going to spend as much as $60 million of his own money on long television commercials that he called "infomercials." He would also appear on the upcoming nationally televised debates with Bush and Clinton. Would Perot's message come across? Could he come from behind and create the biggest surprise of all?

Ross Perot's "October Surprise" drastically changed the nature of the campaign at the last moment.

Opposite:
On October 1, 1992—with only four weeks left in the campaign— Ross Perot officially declared himself to be a candidate for president.

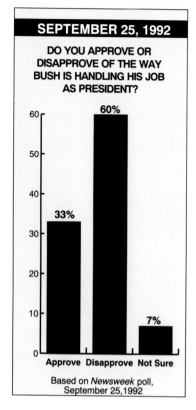

SEPTEMBER 25, 1992

DO YOU APPROVE OR DISAPPROVE OF THE WAY BUSH IS HANDLING HIS JOB AS PRESIDENT?

Based on *Newsweek* poll, September 25, 1992

The President in Trouble

The race that Perot rejoined was not going well for President Bush. A week after his party's convention, George Bush was again way down in the polls. The sticking point with the voters was the economy. How was he going to improve it? Why should voters believe any new plans he proposed when he had been in office for almost four years without setting things right?

Bush also seemed to make a few key misstatements that didn't sit well with voters. One of the most notable was his comment that the economy wasn't "as bad as it seemed" and that things were "about to get better." In his campaign commercials, Clinton jumped on Bush for this. "If Bush doesn't understand the problem, how can he solve it?" was the governor's response.

The economic mess may or may not have been the president's fault, but even people who had voted for Bush four years ago were blaming him for the recession. For a while, he pressed the hard-line "family values" theme that

How the President Is Elected

There are actually not one but fifty elections for president of the United States—a separate contest in each state. In reality, American voters only indirectly vote for their candidate. They choose "electors"—people named by the parties—who are pledged to vote for their candidate in a representative body called the Electoral College. (In most states, only the candidates' names, not the electors' names, appear on the ballot.)

The number of electors each state has in the Electoral College equals the number of senators and representatives it sends to Congress. California, for example, a big state, has two senators and fifty-two members in the House of Representatives, so it has fifty-four electors in the Electoral College. Vermont, with two senators and only one member of the House, has three electors.

The winning candidate in almost every state gets *all* of that state's electoral votes, even if the candidate gets only a few more votes in the state than does his or her opponent. Whichever candidate gets 270 of the total of 538 electoral votes nationwide becomes president.

What happens if no candidate gets 270 electoral votes? This can occur if there are more than two major candidates running, as was the case in the 1992 elections. For example, if Ross Perot had won just enough electoral votes to prevent either George Bush or Bill Clinton from getting the necessary 270 votes, no winner would have been declared on November 3. In such a case, the U.S. House of Representatives would have chosen the next president from among the three leading candidates, with each state delegation having one vote.

was sounded at the Republican convention, but that tactic had made women voters—including many Republicans—angry. They felt that many of those "family values" sentiments were an attack on all working mothers and single parents (most of whom were women). Bush soon dropped the issue.

Clinton Stays Ahead

Meanwhile, Bill Clinton continued to remind voters that unemployment was stuck at 7.5 percent. The governor repeated that he stood for "change," driving home what the polls said voters clearly wanted.

Clinton also questioned what he said were conflicts between what the president said and what he did. For example, Bush had vetoed a bill that would have required businesses to grant employees unpaid leave to deal with family matters, such as the birth of a baby. How could Bush be for "family values" when he prevented Congress from helping families this way? Bush replied that the bill was faulty and would hurt businesses by cutting back on jobs.

Clinton also reminded audiences that Bush had gone back on his "no new taxes" pledge. But Clinton had a problem about whether his own word could be trusted. The governor offered different versions on how he avoided military service during the Vietnam War. Republicans said this showed that Bill Clinton lacked the right "character" to be president and that he couldn't be trusted to tell the truth. George Bush made the issues of "character" and "trust"—and Clinton's patriotism—central to his campaign.

The Debates

Television was playing a big part in the campaign. Besides the usual political commercials, the candidates were appearing on every talk show that would have them. They

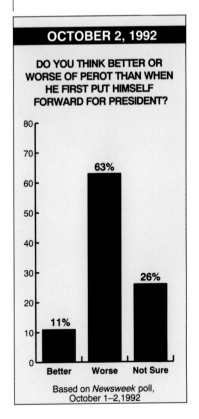

OCTOBER 2, 1992

DO YOU THINK BETTER OR WORSE OF PEROT THAN WHEN HE FIRST PUT HIMSELF FORWARD FOR PRESIDENT?

Better 11%
Worse 63%
Not Sure 26%

Based on *Newsweek* poll, October 1–2, 1992

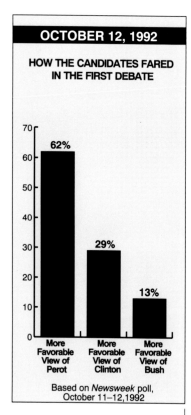

OCTOBER 12, 1992

HOW THE CANDIDATES FARED IN THE FIRST DEBATE

Based on *Newsweek* poll, October 11–12, 1992

even showed up on MTV. But the appearances that were thought to be especially important for Bush were the nationally televised debates.

A series of three presidential debates (and one vice-presidential debate) began on Sunday night, October 11. Far behind in the polls with three weeks to go, George Bush needed to use the debates to turn his campaign around. On the first night, the president did not get the clear victory he needed. He raised the "character" issue, but with little effect. The polls showed that it was the economy voters cared most about.

Bush then tried a surprise. He said that if he were reelected, he would appoint Jim Baker, former secretary of state, to look after the economy. But this plan backfired. Many people thought the president himself should take charge of the economy.

Aware of his big lead, Clinton worked hard to simply avoid making any big mistakes. He played it safe, careful to reply to anything negative George Bush said about him.

The man who looked best on television was Ross Perot. He got viewers on his side by poking fun at Washington politicians. When asked if his lack of political experience would hurt him, Perot turned the question to his advantage. "You're right; I don't have experience," he said. "I don't have any experience in running up a four-trillion-dollar debt."

Perot also began to set himself off from the other candidates with his lengthy political ads. Bush and Clinton ran the usual short spots with slogans. But Perot ran several thirty-minute commercials, some of which were full of facts and figures, charts, and graphs. Many voters watched and liked these commercials, and Perot's standing in the polls moved up to 15 percent.

After the candidates for vice president had a somewhat angry debate, Bush, Clinton, and Perot squared off two more times. Bush still could not get the boost he needed. Clinton fared especially well in the second debate, in which the candidates fielded questions from a studio audience. But if there was any winner, it was Perot, whose support grew to about 20 percent. His rise took support away from Clinton, whose lead over George Bush narrowed by almost as much as Perot's gain. Still, in the states with the largest number of electoral votes, the Arkansas governor held onto a strong lead.

The Issues

Before the debates, it seemed that personalities, slogans, and name-calling were taking over the race. But the debates were effective in convincing the candidates to concentrate on the issues. From October on, it seemed that the candidates, especially Bush and Clinton, took firmer positions on many issues that voters cared about.

Aside from calling for a balanced budget, Perot was not specific on the changes he would make if elected. The government should be run like a business, he said. If he won, he promised to call together the experts on every subject to come up with the best plans, and then put them into effect.

To move the economy, President Bush called for tax cuts for everyone. He said he would limit government spending and introduce tax measures that would get businesses to expand, thus creating jobs. He claimed that Clinton would "tax and spend," the charge Republicans had been making about Democrats for many years.

Clinton called for spending more money on those things that would make America economically stronger, such as education, roads, and bridges. He also wanted a more active government to help industries threatened by foreign competition. He planned to raise money through higher taxes on the wealthy and by taxing profits earned by foreign companies in this country.

On education, Bush said that Americans should be able to choose any school for a child—public or private—with

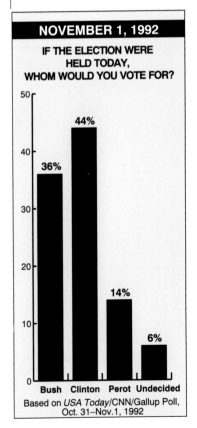

NOVEMBER 1, 1992

IF THE ELECTION WERE HELD TODAY, WHOM WOULD YOU VOTE FOR?

Based on *USA Today*/CNN/Gallup Poll, Oct. 31–Nov.1, 1992

the government paying for it. Clinton was against government funds for private schools, but he agreed that parents should be able to choose among public schools.

Clinton said abortion should be a matter of choice. Bush ran on a platform that favored a constitutional amendment allowing states to ban abortions.

Both candidates called for health-care reforms. Clinton advocated universal health insurance, provided by employers or through a government pool. Bush proposed tax credits to help people pay for health insurance.

The president reminded voters that the Cold War had ended while he was in office, and he said that his policy of keeping America's military strong had helped to stop communism. Bill Clinton pointed out that in the 1990s, with communism no longer a threat, America's economy would be the heart of its strength. He wanted bigger cuts in the military so that more could be spent on boosting the economy. He also raised questions about whether Bush had invited the Gulf War by giving Saddam Hussein the impression that his aggressive policies would not be met by force.

Bush called Clinton and Gore environmental "extremists" for stressing nature too much at the expense of jobs. Clinton said that there was no reason the two concerns couldn't be kept in balance.

The candidates talked little of how they would pay for their programs. They virtually ignored talk of urban problems, the poor, and racial minorities. Instead, they kept stressing what they would do for the middle class.

Strange Doings

The last two weeks saw a hectic scramble for preelection positioning. Ross Perot suddenly got sidetracked when he lashed out at what he called "Republican dirty tricks." He claimed that he had dropped out of the race in July because of a plot by Republicans to disrupt his daughter's wedding, but he offered no proof. The Bush campaign called Perot's charges "loony."

Clinton was careful not to get involved as Bush and Perot went at each other. It seemed like a break for the governor, who could talk about the issues while the others bickered.

Down to the Wire

As Election Day approached, each candidate had to decide where he could best spend his time and money. Since Richard Nixon's election in 1968, Republicans had won in the South except for 1976, when Jimmy Carter, a southerner, was the Democratic nominee. But with two moderate southerners on the Democratic ticket in 1992, the electoral votes of many southern states appeared to be headed for the Democratic forces.

George Bush needed to spend precious time and money campaigning in places like Texas, Florida, and North Carolina, which in 1988 he had won easily. With Clinton leading in New Jersey, Bush had to visit there frequently, too. Ohio and Michigan were other battlegrounds that the president had to visit, states in which Republicans traditionally had leads.

Clinton held a big lead in New York and California. This gave him the luxury of going after states where the race was close, but which had not recently voted Democratic. In the West he visited Colorado and Montana. He, too, crisscrossed North Carolina, stumped in Texas and New Jersey, and spoke in the Midwest.

November 3: The People Decide

Clinton was right: America did want change. On Tuesday, November 3, 1992, Bill Clinton was elected president with 370 electoral votes to George Bush's 168. Perot got none, but he did win about 19 percent of the popular vote, the most for a third-party candidate since Teddy

Roosevelt in 1912. Clinton received 43 percent of the popular vote, and Bush received 38 percent.

The three-way race meant that Clinton was elected without a majority of the popular vote. It also raised questions about the future of the two-party system. Was Perot's showing a fluke, brought on by bad economic times? Or was it the beginning of a trend? Perot himself did not rule out a bid for the presidency in 1996.

The economy was the issue that won the race for Clinton. He ran strongest in the Northeast and in California, where unemployment was the highest. His hard campaigning in the states where the race was close also paid off. He won states such as Georgia, New Jersey, and Ohio that were up for grabs until the final hours. Bush took Florida and Texas, states he had to win, as well as

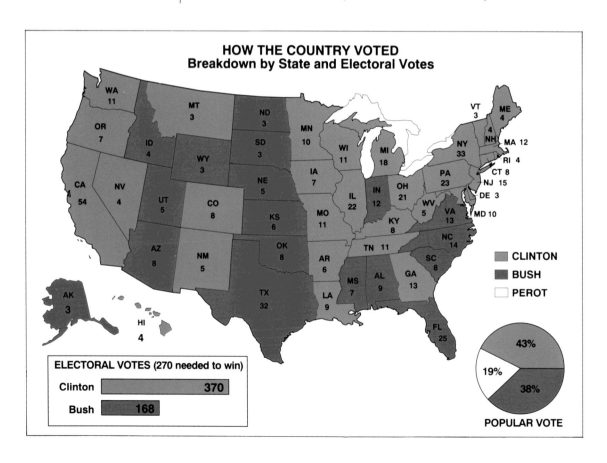

HOW THE COUNTRY VOTED
Breakdown by State and Electoral Votes

CLINTON
BUSH
PEROT

43%
19%
38%

POPULAR VOTE

ELECTORAL VOTES (270 needed to win)

Clinton 370
Bush 168

traditionally Republican states such as Indiana and Nebraska. But he did not win enough everywhere else.

The election also brought changes to Congress. Fed-up voters did not, as some had predicted, turn all their incumbent senators and representatives out of office. But they did choose over one hundred new members of Congress. Many were women and other minorities, including the first black woman senator, Democrat Carol Moseley Braun of Illinois. And fourteen states voted to limit the number of terms senators and representatives could serve.

Problems Ahead

President-elect Bill Clinton had little time to enjoy his victory. He faced enormous problems. With a lagging economy, a growing budget deficit, and unmet social needs, something had to give. Because the Democrats did well in all the local elections, both the House and Senate would have Democratic majorities. That meant a Democratic president would have no excuses for inaction. Clinton pledged to make his first "hundred days" both productive and effective.

When he claimed victory on election night, Clinton made it clear that none of these problems could be solved unless the wounds of the rough campaign could be healed. His first job, he said, would begin by bringing together a "re-United States." It seemed that Dan Quayle joined Clinton somewhat in the effort. In his concession speech, Quayle said of Clinton, "If he runs the country as well as he ran his campaign, we'll be okay."

Even though guiding America for the next four years would not be easy, America seemed ready to have Bill Clinton try.

Chronology

1990 — The economy in the United States starts to decline, leading to a recession by the fall of 1991. Unemployment rates are very high as many jobs are lost.

March 6, 1991 — President Bush declares victory in Operation Desert Storm. His popularity is at an all-time high.

Fall 1991 — The Senate's handling of Clarence Thomas's Supreme Court nomination angers many voters, especially women.

Several Democrats declare their bid for president, including Bill Clinton, Bob Kerrey, Tom Harkin, Paul Tsongas, and Jerry Brown.

February 12, 1992 — George Bush formally enters the race for president.

February 18, 1992 — In the New Hampshire primary, Bush wins, but Pat Buchanan gets 37 percent of the vote. Paul Tsongas is the Democratic winner.

February 20, 1992 — Ross Perot appears on "Larry King Live" and says he will run for president if he can get his name on the ballot in all fifty states.

March 10, 1992 — Clinton wins big on Super Tuesday, taking nine states.

March 1992 — Bob Kerrey, Tom Harkin, and Paul Tsongas drop out of the Democratic race, citing dwindling campaign funds.

June 6, 1992 — Clinton wins enough delegates to assure his nomination.

July 13, 1992 — The Democratic convention opens in New York City. A Clinton-Gore ticket is chosen.

July 16, 1992 — Perot, although only an unofficial candidate, drops out of the race for president.

August 17, 1992 — The Republican convention opens in Houston, Texas, supporting George Bush and Dan Quayle.

October 1, 1992 — Ross Perot reenters the race as an official candidate.

October 11, 1992 — The first of the three presidential debates is held.

November 3, 1992 — Bill Clinton is elected president, but without a popular majority.

For Further Reading

Hargrove, J. *Presidential Elections*. Chicago: Childrens Press, 1990.

Johnson, Mary. *The President*. Austin: Raintree Steck-Vaughn, 1992.

Scher, Linda. *The Vote*. Austin: Raintree Steck-Vaughn, 1992.

Schlesinger, Arthur M., Jr., ed. *History of American Presidential Elections*. Broomall: Chelsea House, 1990.

Index

Acknowledgments and photo credits

Cover (left to right): Wide World Photos, © Cynthia Johnson/Gamma-Liaison, Wide World Photos; pp. 4, 14, 18, 26, 29, 30, 32, 33, 34, 37, 38: AP/Wide World Photos; p. 6: © Carolyn Schaefer/Peter B. Kaplan/Gamma-Liaison; pp. 8, 28, 41, 42, 47 (top and bottom): B. Markel/Gamma-Liaison; p. 9: © Georges Merillon/Gamma-Liaison; p. 10: © Paul S. Howell/Gamma-Liaison; pp. 12, 35: Wide World Photos; p. 15: © Dickman/Gamma-Liaison; pp. 17, 50 (left), 51 (bottom): © Dirck Halstead/Gamma-Liaison; p. 31 (top): © Cynthia Johnson/Gamma-Liaison; p. 31 (bottom): Jim Bourg/Gamma-Liaison; p. 39: U.S. Mint, Bureau of Engraving and Printing; pp. 46 and inset, 50 (right), 51 (top): © Joe Traver/Gamma-Liaison; p.52: © David Woo/Gamma-Liaison.
Charts and maps by Sandra Burr.